Y0-CDN-518

Self Help

WOMEN
CONNECTING WITH
WOMEN

Study Guide
with Leader's Notes

Equipping Women for
Friend-to-Friend Support
and Mentoring

Verna Birkey

WINEPRESS WP PUBLISHING

Women Connecting with Women Study Guide
© 1998 by Verna Birkey

Published by:
WinePress Publishing
PO Box 1406
Mukilteo, WA 98275

Unless otherwise indicated, Scripture references are from the Holy Bible, New International Version, copyright 1973, 1978, 1984 by the International Bible Society.

Verses marked AMP are taken from The Amplified Bible, Old Testament, Copyright © 1965 and 1987 by The Zondervan Corporation, and from The Amplified New Testament, Copyright © 1954, 1958, 1987 by The Lockman Foundation. Used by permission.

Verses marked NKJV are taken from the New King James Version, Copyright © 1979, 1980, 1982 by Thomas Nelson, Inc., Publishers. Used by permission.

Verses marked KJV are taken from the King James Version of the Bible.

Scripture references marked Phillips are from J. B. Phillips: The New Testament in Modern English, copyright © 1958, 1960, 1972 Macmillan Publishing Co., Inc.

Verses marked NASB are taken from the New American Standard Bible, © 1960, 1963, 1968, 1971, 1972, 1973, 1975, 1977 by The Lockman Foundation. Used by permission.

Printed in the United States of America.

ISBN 1-57921-106-2
Library of Congress Catalog Card Number: 98-60297

Contents

Part IV—Nourishing Others Through People-Helping

Before You Begin

*L*inx: *Women Connecting with Women* is full of life-changing concepts that could mean a fuller, richer life in Christ for you and for those around you. This *Study Guide,* a companion to the text, is designed to help you take what you read through your mind, into your heart, and out into your daily responses. It guides you in thinking through each chapter and provides a place to respond. You will need the textbook *Linx: Women Connecting with Women* in order to use this *Study Guide.*

Our two key words in *Linx* are *equipping* and *connecting.* In today's broken world women are longing for warm relationships. At times we've all reached out for understanding, only to be disappointed. Equipping women before they connect with one another leads to more supportive, grace-giving relationships. My passion in this book is to equip each member of the body to become someone who understands, accepts, hears, knows, and believes in another.

Beginning with chapter 2 each chapter is divided into five days. We suggest that you read the text, study the pages designated and answer the *Study Guide* questions each day for five days. This will spread the study through most of the week and give you time to digest and think about the various concepts presented.

Page numbers throughout refer to the textbook unless otherwise noted.

How to Use This Study Guide

This *Study Guide* is designed as a companion to the textbook, *Linx: Women Connecting with Women.*

For Individual Study, for Personal Growth

Read a chapter from the textbook each week, highlighting ideas relevant to you and answering the questions in this *Study Guide*. Read with Bible in hand, looking up the Scriptures, marking them in your Bible.

For Group Study, to Help Others

You can benefit greatly from individual study of *Linx: Women Connecting with Women*; but studying with a small group, or even with one other person, can greatly enhance that blessing. This time together can also be the beginning of some warm, personal connections with understanding, caring friends. Beginning on page 77 of this Study Guide you will find helpful "Leader's Notes"—suggestions for discussion and interaction, whether with one other person or a larger group.

- Reading the textbook and working through each chapter of the *Study Guide* with one or two other persons who meet in your home is a simple and easy way to reach out to others.
- Or, use the books in small group Sunday or weekday classes.
- Make *Linx* the basis for a church-wide women's study. Women can read the chapter at home and answer the questions, then come together, first in small groups for discussion and then all together for a "wrap-up" by a leader/teacher. Wrap-up suggestions are given in the "Leader's Notes."

Getting to Know You

These questions are provided for groups, or they may even be used as you study with one or two other persons. They are meant to break the ice and help you get acquainted.

Between Linx Practicing and Journaling

Beginning with chapter 2 in the textbook, you will find "Practicing and Journaling" suggestions at the end of each chapter. In this *Study Guide* they come at the beginning of the next chapter so that you may work on them during the week and jot some notes on what you have done. We strongly encourage you to make this a priority, an application target for the week. This will help you to internalize the truth that will set you free. It will be one more step in transforming your life so that you can better manifest the life of Jesus and experience the joy of personal freedom in Him. Writing each week how you have applied the *Linx* teaching can serve as a journal to look back at your progress, giving you a written history of your growth and progress. It can also serve as a springboard for sharing, if you are studying with a small group.

Thoughts to Remember

At the end of each chapter the "Thoughts to Remember" section in the textbook provides a memory verse and a succinct summary statement of the main thrust of that chapter. We recommend that you write these on a card each week and carry the card with you. Memorize both the scripture and the statement, and thus put them to work in your daily life.

1

Needed: Safe People, Safe Places

Getting to Know You

If you are studying in a group, tell your name and your favorite way to spend free time.

Needed: Safe People, Safe Places (Pages 13-15 in textbook)

1. In what ways was the uncle not a grace giver and a safe person?

2. In what way was Verna's dad's dad not a grace giver? That is, how did he fail to create a safe environment for his son?

3. What are some of our deep soul hungers?

4. We all have a deep desire to connect with another. What do we want from those with whom we link?

5. Our two key words are _____ and
   _____.

Key Word: Connecting (Pages 15-18)
1. Women need connection with other women because:

2. What does Paul urge us to do in 1 Thessalonians 5:11 and 14?

3. Read Hannah's story on page 16. How was Verna a grace giver to her?

4. What kind of confused and twisted thinking do women need to be released from? How can these people best be helped?

Key Word: Equipping (Pages 18-23)
1. Equipping ourselves with better people-relating skills will make our _____ much deeper and more _____.

2. Read Titus 2:3–4. What was Titus to do for the older women?

3. What were the older women to do for the younger women?

4. How do you feel Titus 2:3–5 relates to you at this stage of your life?

5. Where would you place yourself on the scale of "confident or reluctant"?

    Confident . . . . .Reluctant

The Work of Encouragement (Pages 22-23)
1. How would you define "older" and "younger" as they relate to friend-to-friend mentoring?

2. At this point in your thinking, in what area do you see yourself as "older"—that is, able to encourage or teach a "younger."

A Challenge to Get Involved (Pages 23-29)
1. Consider these two statements from Henry Blackaby: God is _____ at work around _____ and God _____ us to join Him in what He is _____.

2. Blackaby goes on to say that getting involved in what God is doing requires _____ and _____ and results in having to make major _____ in our _____.

3. How was this true for Moses?

For Verna?

4. What are some major adjustments you might have to make to join God in what He wants to do through you?

2

Free to Nourish Others

Getting to Know You

    When you were growing up, what person made you feel best about yourself? Why?

Review Thoughts to Remember (Page 28)

DAY 1 (PAGES 31-35 IN TEXTBOOK)

1. What was the basis for Verna's crying at that three-day seminar?

Nourishing Others Is God's Idea

2. Read Ephesians 5:28–29 and 1 Thessalonians 5:11. What does God want us to do for one another?

3. Read John 1:14. How did Jesus nourish people?

4. How was grace and truth shown to the woman taken in adultery and to her accusers? (John 8:3–11)

5. What do you learn from the way Jesus and Paul nourished others?

Day 2 (Pages 35-38)

1. If you knew that God had worked miracles through Elijah and then heard he was so depressed that he wanted to die, what might your first thoughts have been? How would you have helped him with his problem? (The story is in 1 Kings 17–19.)

2. What did God say Elijah needed most at this time?

3. When might it be appropriate to share a scripture or gentle counsel with one in pain or depression?

4. How was grace and truth fleshed out in one of Jesus' representatives? (Page 37)

Day 3 (Pages 38-42)

Women Are to Nourish Other Women

1. Read Titus 2:1–5. What is the "Titus 2 business" for women?

2. What do you learn of a mentoring relationship from Naomi and Ruth? (Ruth 1 and 3:1–6)

3. Imagine some of the conversation that might have occurred between Mary and Elizabeth. (Luke 1:39–45)

4. Jot down some of your insights from reading "Younger Women Want to Connect." Do you have an experience you could share?

Day 4 (Pages 42-46)

Guidelines for Nourishing Others

1. Read 1 Peter 5:3. What do we mean when we say we are to be "God with skin on" and what do we not mean?

2. Read 1 John 2:1(NKJV). One way to be "God with skin on" is to be an advocate like Jesus. What is an advocate?

3. How was Jesus an advocate for Mary? (Mark 14:3–9)

4. Tell of a time when someone was an advocate for you or you were an advocate for another?

Day 5 (Pages 46-52)

1. Read John 14:16, 26; 15:26; and 16:7 (AMP). Describe a paraclete.

2. What are some ways to come alongside another
    —As an encourager?

    —As a support person?

    —As a helper?

3. Read Psalm 46:1. Who is the only true, unfailing, and safe refuge?

    How can you be a refuge or safe person to another?

3

Free to Be Nourished

Getting to Know You
If you had the whole day to spend however you wanted, what would you do?

Review Thoughts to Remember (Page 52)

Between Linx Practicing and Journaling (Page 52)
Plan to do something this week to nourish another—spouse, child, friend. Be an advocate, a paraclete (support, encourage, help), or a refuge. Write out one thing you did and how the person responded.

Day 1 (Pages 53-57)

God Made Us with a Need for Nourishment
1. Verna realized that, though her *primary* purpose at the high school was to show the girls what Jesus is like, her impatient spirit did the opposite. What was the cause and what did she need to do about it?

2. In what areas do you need to give some attention to nourishing yourself in order to represent Him well? What will you choose to do about it?

3. Read Matthew 22:37–39 and 1 John 3:23; 4:9–11, 21. God made us with two vacuums in the soul. What are they and how are they to be nourished?

Day 2 (Pages 57-60)

The Family: God's Primary Place of Nourishment
1. What was God's original plan for our nourishment needs to be met on the human level?

What happened to ruin this plan and what was the result?

Take Responsibility to Be Nurtured
2. If we were not properly nourished as children, what must we do about it now?

3. Why is it right and necessary to be sure that we ourselves are well nourished?

4. How did Jesus take responsibility for his own nourishment?

What nourishment did He receive from others? (See John 12:1–8.)

DAY 3 (PAGES 61-68)

Reach Out for Nourishment from God

1. Our primary source of nourishment is God. People, things, and activities are to be a supplementary source. The danger is to make things primary and God the supplement. What might you be looking to as a primary source of nourishment rather than God?

2. Read Luke 5:16 and John 4:32–34. What were Jesus' major sources of nourishment?

3. Read John 1:12, 3:36 and Ephesians 2:8–9. How can one become God's child? Is doing good and being good adequate to assure us a place in heaven? Do you have assurance that you are a child of God?

4. Read Jeremiah 15:16 and Psalm 119:11, 50, 165. Why is spending time regularly in the Word important?

Day 4 (Pages 68-71)

Reach Out for Activities That Nourish

1. What kinds of activities nourish you; that is, what gives you strength, refreshes you emotionally, and gives you energy?

2. Read Genesis 2:8–25. What did God provide as soul nourishment for Adam and Eve?

3. What insights did you gain from *Lord Bacon* or other examples?

4. Which of the warnings about activities that nourish do you need to give attention to?

Day 5 (Pages 72-76)

Reach Out for Nourishment from Others

1. How did Paul reach out for nourishment from others? (2 Timothy 4:9–11)

2. It's not selfish to consider our own needs—it's being _____.
   The Bible says that _____ and
   _____ are to be denied; the need for
   relationship with others is emphasized. What are the motives that make
   the difference?

3. What are three cautions to consider when reaching out to others?

4. Consider where you need to take more initiative, and possibly some
   risks, to receive nourishment from others. Will you choose now to do
   so? Do you have a person in mind?

4

Origins of Malnourishment

Getting to Know You

What sorts of activities absolutely drain the life out of you. On the other hand, what gives you energy?

Review Thoughts to Remember (Page 76)

Between Linx Practicing and Journaling (Page 76)

Plan to do something this week just to nourish yourself. Write what you did, how others responded, and how you felt about it.

DAY 1 (PAGES 79-86 IN TEXTBOOK)

Sin Disrupted God's Plan

1. What is the new principle that sin introduced that has been plaguing us all since Adam and Eve? Describe what it sounds like.

2. How did you feel about Judy pouring out her anger to the Lord with such strength and accusation? Why was she so needy, so hungry for love?

What does Psalm 62:8 say about what and how we share with the Lord?

Causes of Malnourishment (Pages 81)

3. How nourishing was your family environment? Rate it on a scale of 1 to 10, with 10 being the most nourishing.
   What is one way you were nourished?

4. Describe some of the pain that resulted from lack of nourishment and a bit about how it affected you. (Optional)

Day 2 (Pages 86-89)

Hope and Healing for the Malnourished

1. How did Joseph's brothers feel about him and treat him? (Genesis 37)

2. What were some of Joseph's other misfortunes/adversities? (Genesis 39–41)

3. Joseph did two things to find healing from these bruises. What were they?

4. Explain the difference between excusing and forgiving.

Day 3 (Pages 89-91)

1. Genesis 42–45 cover Joseph's careful, wise plan as he seeks to move his brothers to full forgiveness and reconciliation. For reconciliation the brothers needed to:

    (1) face their sinful _____, (2) feel the _____ they caused him, (3) _____, and (4) prove themselves_____.

2. Joseph learned to take responsibility for his own _____, but not for their _____. In fact, he said, "You meant _____ against me. . . . " (Genesis 50:20, NKJV)

3. If you have come from an unhealthy family where there was deceit, lying, selfishness, neglect, abuse from parents, and abuse, hatred, jealousy, and rejections from siblings or others, are you willing to take Joseph's way of healing?

    a) Keep your focus on the Lord—His _____, His _____, and His good _____ for your life.

    b) _____ those who have wronged you, acknowledging their _____ against you and choosing to _____ them.

4. Is there someone in your life you need to forgive? Are you willing to take that step now?

Day 4 (Pages 91-96)

Malnourishment Fosters Wrong Thinking
1. Warning lights in cars as well as in our _____ signal us that something is _____ and needs _____.

2. Using the pear diagram, explain how we form flesh patterns.

3. What negative conclusion have you drawn about yourself? What typical sentence do you tend to say to yourself about it?

4. We can so easily give the devil a _____ and then let it develop into a flesh pattern. This is walking according to the_____ and not according to the _____. (See Ephesians 4:27 and Romans 8:4–5.) Have you identified a flesh pattern that you need to replace by walking in the power of the Spirit?

Day 5 (Pages 96-100)

1. So that we can experience the truth that makes us free, we need to have our wrong thinking exposed. What are three major means the Lord uses to enlighten us?

2. Read 2 Samuel 12:1–14. How did God expose David's wrong thinking and behavior?

3. How can you expose this hurtful thinking in your life?

4. Choose one of these prayers to pray: Psalm 139:23–24 (NASB) or Psalm 18:28 (KJV).

5. Read 2 Corinthians 10:5 (KJV) and Romans 12:2 (KJV). Share how you have taken "wrong thoughts captive" or "renewed your mind."

5

Hurtful, Twisted Thinking

Getting to Know You
Share your favorite childhood memory.

Review Thoughts to Remember (Page 100)

Between Linx Practicing and Journaling (Page 100)
Review "Traits of a Healthy Family" and put a check by one or two that you need to work on. Write a statement about what you plan to do about it this week.

DAY 1 (PAGES 101-104 IN TEXTBOOK)

Changing Our Hurtful Thinking
1. Why was Diane inwardly fuming? What gave her peace even though the circumstances were unchanged?

2. What are four things we can do to change our hurtful thinking?

3. Read Proverbs 16:24 and 18:21. What insights are in these verses in regard to the importance of what we say?

4. Explain the ABCs of our emotions. What does each letter represent?

Day 2 (Pages 104-106)

1. From Numbers 13:1–14:10 notice the different responses of the two and the ten, though they were reporting on the same event.

2. What was the self-talk (and other talk) and the resultant feelings of the ten?

   What did their negative thinking lead to?

3. What was the self-talk (and other talk) of the two and their resultant feelings?

4. Read Isaiah 26:3. To whom does God promise perfect peace? Underline this verse in your Bible.

DAY 3 (PAGES 106-111)

Results of Malnourishment

1. Describe the "all-or-nothing" attitude. How might it be expressed?

2. Give a statement that might describe how one who is perfectionistic in relationships thinks?

3. What is one example of truth out of balance?

4. Have you identified in yourself a tendency toward any "all-or-nothing" characteristics? If so, which one?

DAY 4 (PAGES 111-116)

1. Where does the "take charge" mentality often come from?

2. What were some factors that encouraged Lana to become a take-charge person, a fixer, and enabler?

3. Review some of the common thoughts/statements of distorted views of self, others, or God. Do you relate to any of them?

4. Have you had some distorted views about how the Christian life works? If so, what are some?

DAY 5 (PAGES 116-119)

How Can We Change These Patterns?
1. Why is it important to identify and correct our distortions of truth?

2. Which distortion of truth do you tend to struggle with? Write a plan for dealing with this.

3. Mark Psalm 139:23–24 in your Bible. Pray this prayer and trust the Lord to work in you to change these wrong thoughts.

4. To summarize and personalize this chapter: Think—what is a typical comment you often make to yourself when you feel that you have failed at something?

6

Dealing with Negative Self-Talk

Getting to Know You

When you were a child, what did you want to be or do when you grew up?

Review Thoughts to Remember (Page 119)

Between Linx Practicing and Journaling (Page 119)

What event happened this week that resulted in your feeling sad or happy? What did you say to yourself about it. What changes could you make in your self-talk that would cause positive changes in your attitude or feelings?

DAY 1 (PAGES 121-126 IN TEXTBOOK)

1. In brief, what can we do to be freed from the tyranny of negative self-talk? Even though it sounds simple, it takes time and hard work. It's a process.

Wrong Behavior Is Based on Flawed Thinking
2. What do the letters A + D = E mean?

    Contrast them with A + B = C.

3. What might have been some of Betty Jean's negative self-talk that was causing her depression?

4. Since her circumstances had not changed, what did change? Be specific.

DAY 2 (PAGES 127-129)

The Importance of Renewing the Mind
1. Read in Job 1:1–22 about the tragedies in Job's life. When he heard the terrible news from the four servants, what did he do?

2. What do you think you might think or say in the midst of such tragedies?

3. After Job worshiped, what was his self-talk or other-talk? (verse 21)

4. Job did not charge God with wrongdoing. Instead, in effect, he was saying, "God owes me _____. He's in _____ and I choose to trust His _____, goodness, _____, and power. His attitude was one of heart _____ and confident _____.

DAY 3 (PAGES 129-133)

1. When we say from the heart, "God . . . is the blessed controller of all things," what are we acknowledging?

2. Saying, "God . . . is the Blessed Controller of all things," is positive self-talk at its best. Believing it produces a positive change in our thoughts and consequently in our E_____.

3. Based on Psalm 84:11, what could have been Jessica's new, positive self talk (**D**)? (Page 130)

   As a result, what might have been her E?

4. How did Sara's interpretation of the events of her childhood put negative content into her belief system?

DAY 4 (PAGES 133-137)

1. How can you use self-talk to overcome a problem or accept one of life's trials?

2. Review the seven suggestions for fighting the battle for the mind. Which do you feel you need to work on most? Explain.

3. Read Hebrews 13:5–6 and Zechariah 4:6. Build what you say to yourself on what God says. And remember that the Holy Spirit wants to empower you to change. Talk to Him about it. What method have you used to retrain your wrong thoughts? Perhaps your method could be useful to others.

Helps for Correcting Twisted Thinking

4. Browse through this section and see if some of these might be of help to you in retraining your thoughts. Pray about using some of these to help others correct their thinking.

DAY 5 (PAGES 137-140)

Clarifying the Thought-Changing Process

1. Remember it's not the _____ but our thoughts about it that create our _____ and affect our behavior. (Proverbs 23:7, NKJV)

2. Why does the dual tape recorder give a better picture of this thought-changing process than the single tape recorder?

3. Read again my old negative tape message and then my new truth tape based on 2 Timothy 1:12 (page 139). Personalize this for your own need. Or, write a new positive self-talk message using a scripture verse, a verse of song, or a statement of truth that counters the negative self-talk messages you tend to play from time to time.

7

Boundaries

Getting to Know You
What rules or guidelines do you remember from your home as a child? How did you respond?

Review Thoughts to Remember (Page 140)

Between Linx Practicing and Journaling (Page 140)
During the next three weeks be aware of your self-talk. Fill in the chart, possibly beginning with C.

SELF-TALK CHART

A	B	C	D	E
Activating event	Beliefs: negative self-talk	Consequences: feelings, emotions	Declared truth: positive self-talk	changed Emotions

We find many references in scripture of people "talking to themselves." Some are giving positive input, some negative. Look up some of these scriptures and notice the self-talk. Choose to memorize one verse. Write it on a card to carry with you. Psalms 14:1; 16:6–8; 57:7–8; 73; 77; 116:7; Lamentations 3:19–26; Habakkuk 3:17–19.

DAY 1 (PAGES 145-148 IN TEXTBOOK)

1. What did you learn about drawing boundaries from the story of Amy and Belva? Read John 21:19–22.

What Is a Boundary?
2. Describe what a boundary is.

3. List some specific things that belong to the other person and some specific things that belong to you.

4. Read Galatians 6:2 and 5. How does "Each one should carry his own load" apply to boundaries?

DAY 2 (PAGES 148-153)

Jesus and Boundaries
1. Read Luke 10:38–42. Why do you think Jesus didn't tell Mary to help Martha?

2. What might have been some of Martha's self-talk that caused her feeling of frustration with Mary? Whose property was Martha's frustration?

Violated Boundaries

3. Can you give an example of someone violating your boundaries?

4. What is one of the first lessons that dedicated, serving people need to learn? Why?

Day 3 (Pages 153-157)

Biblical Teaching on Boundaries

1. Read 1 Corinthians 9:3–6; 12–23. What does Paul here make clear about our rights?

2. Read Galatians 1:10. Is it "Christian" to not always please people? Explain.

3. When drawing boundaries, what other factor must I also consider according to Colossians 3:14?

4. What are three basic principles for setting limits? (See 1 Corinthians 10:23–24 and 31–33, and Galatians 6:10, AMP.) Can you illustrate each of these?

Day 4 (Pages 157-162)

Internal and External Boundaries

1. What is an "internal boundary"? According to Proverbs 25:28 what is a person without internal boundaries like?

2. What factors encouraged Jennifer to be emotionally drawn to the house foreman?

   What was one thing that gave her release and a new power to draw boundaries and resist the temptation?

3. What were some of Natalie's personal external boundaries?

Warning Signals

4. Review the warning signals. Do you see any indications that you may need to give more attention to drawing some proper boundaries? If so, what are they?

Day 5 (Pages 163-167)

Deterrents to Setting Boundaries

1. Have you failed to draw boundaries because of wrong thinking, fear, or pressure from others? Explain.

2. Have you thought it is wrong to draw limits because of wrong teaching or out-of-balance emphasis? What was that and how did it affect you?

Benefits of Boundaries

3. Learning the truth about what is my responsibility and what is not my responsibility, and drawing limits accordingly is a wonderful step toward _____.

4. Summarize three areas of freedom.

8

More About Boundaries

Getting to Know You
What kind of mischief did you get into as a child? (Like skipping chores, reading after lights out, etc.)

Review Thoughts to Remember (Page 167)

Between Linx Practicing and Journaling (Page 167)
Continue working on self-talk chart (*Study Guide* page 39).

Day 1 (Pages 169-173)

Consequences of No Boundaries
1. What might have been some of the consequences if Harriet had drawn no boundaries and out of guilt had bought a bigger home to accommodate her unhappy mother?

2. Who loses growth toward maturity when no boundaries are set? Explain.

3. Have you experienced some consequences of not drawing boundaries?

Guidelines for Drawing Boundaries

4. Which of the "Don'ts" do you need to give most attention to?

Day 2 (Pages 174-176)

Ways to Set Limits

1. When might it be wise to set a boundary for physical or emotional distancing?

2. When might you set a boundary limiting the time you spend with another?

3. What might be a proper occasion to suggest a project before getting together again?

4. Share how you have wisely drawn a boundary and explain the result. What might have been the consequences if you had neglected to set the limits?

DAY 3 (PAGES 177-184)

The Scope of Boundaries

1. What are some internal boundaries you need to set for yourself?

2. What are some specific boundaries you need to set in regard to the people in your life—friends, spouse, children, coworkers, neighbors?

3. Are there some boundaries you need to set in regard to your Christian ministry or Christian activities? What are they?

4. Are there some boundaries you need to set in regard to your hobbies? Are you ready to make plans for this?

DAY 4 (PAGES 184-188)

Why Take the Risk?

1. What are the three possible reasons for setting limits?

2. What is the major reason you hesitate about or fail to draw boundaries?

Expect Some Resistance

3. What are some ways people may show their resistance to the limits you set with them?

4. Have you tried to draw a boundary and met with resistance? Please share the situation, the type of resistance, and how you handled it.

Day 5 (Pages 188-193)

Honor Others' Boundaries

1. Can you think of a time when someone would not hear your no? Tell about the situation and your response.

2. Was there a time when you helped someone else say no to you or to another?

Use Godly Wisdom in Setting Boundaries

3. There are times when we must be discerning and careful **not** to set limits. What are they?

4. Read Colossians 3:14 and Ephesians 4:2. What is to be the over-all guideline when we think of setting limits?

9

Conflict Resolution

Getting to Know You
Can you give an example of someone's violation of your boundaries?

Review Thoughts to Remember (Page 193)

Between Linx Practicing and Journaling (Page 193)
1. Fill in third week of the ABC chart (*Study Guide* page 39).

2. Write about a time when you drew a boundary this week, the result it had in you, and the response of the other person. Do you think that you did it in the right way?

DAY 1 (PAGES 195-201)

Sources of Conflict
In your own words explain the following sources of conflict and give an example:
1. Crossed Boundaries

2. Locked Wills

3. Unspoken or Wrong Assumptions

4. Unfulfilled Expectations and Personalization

Day 2 (Pages 201-207)

Sources of Conflict (continued)
1. Share a time when someone or something blocked your goal. Explain how you felt and what happened.

2. Read again "Review Some Significant Points" (page 206) about things Rae Ann felt or did when she was sinned against. What two or three do you feel were most significant in **healing the relationship?**

3. What were some significant things for Rae Ann's **personal help and healing?**

Analyze the Conflict
4. Think back to a time when you had a conflict with another. Which of these seven possible sources of conflict was the issue?

DAY 3 (PAGES 207-213)

Wrong Ways of Responding in Conflict
1. List the four typical wrong ways of responding in conflict and the message each gives.

2. List the four forms the manipulative response style might take.

3. Has any of these four typical wrong responses **by you or to you** affected your life? Explain.

4. Do you tend to respond in one of these ways? Which one?

DAY 4 (PAGES 213-215)

1. "In addition to being ineffective in _____ and not _____ the problem, these wrong response styles tend to _____ the _____ and _____ a proper sense of _____." (Top of page 213)

2. Can you share a time when you were wrongly dealt with in a situation? Which wrong response was it and how did you deal with this conflict?

The "Jesus Way"
3. In what three ways do we find Jesus responding in the midst of conflict?
   A)   John 2:13–17:

   B)   1 Peter 2:23 (KJV):

   C)   John 18:22–23:

DAY 5 (PAGES 215-219)

1. How does Ephesians 4:15 explain the "Jesus Way" of responding in conflict?

2. Many times when wronged by another we tend to isolate, become cool, and draw away from that one. Instead, Matthew 18:15–16 says, "If your brother sins against you, go and _____ _____."

3. What do we mean when we say, "As we speak hard-to-hear truth, we must do it with grace?"

4. How can you incorporate into your own life the "Jesus way" of responding to conflict?

10

Confrontation

Getting to Know You
How many brothers and sisters do you have? What is your birth order? Do you feel it was an advantage or a disadvantage? Why?

Review Thoughts to Remember (Page 219)

Between Linx Practicing and Journaling (Page 219)
Think through and evaluate your conflict areas:
1. With whom do you tend to have the most conflict?

2. Which one of the seven typical sources of conflict initiates your conflicts most frequently?

3. What is your most typical wrong response to conflict? How do you feel you can change that?

Day 1 (Pages 221-226)

1. What were some positive things Jana did? What was Jana's spirit throughout this encounter?

The Importance of Confronting
2. How would you define "confront" in this context?

3. We are to care enough to confront. How does David Augsburger define "Carefronting"?

4. What guidance do Proverbs 20:18 and 24:6 give about confronting?

Day 2 (Pages 226-228)

Guidelines for Confronting
1. What questions should you ask yourself to help you decide whether or not you need to confront?

2. If you sense that confronting is not that important or has no potential for healing, what should you do?

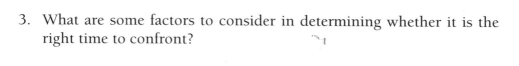
3. What are some factors to consider in determining whether it is the right time to confront?

4. Have you had a time when you tried to confront and it didn't work out well? Can you now think of something you might have done differently?

Day 3 (Pages 228-229)

1. Read Matthew 5:23–24 and 18:15. When there is an issue between two people, who should take the initiative in trying to be reconciled?

2. From 1 Corinthians 11:2, 17–34, what are five elements in the pattern Paul gives for addressing a situation?

3. Is it always necessary and wise to go through all five steps? Explain.

Day 4 (Pages 229-233)

1. In preparing yourself to confront, it's important to give attention to your manner. From Colossians 3:12–15 (Phillips) choose one or two characteristics that seem most important to you.

2. When you attempt to confront, what are some ways the other person may try to sidetrack you?

3. In preparing what you are going to say, what four things are good to incorporate?

4. What do we learn about addressing the situation from the Prodigal Son in Luke 15:11–32?

Day 5 (Pages 233-236)

Balancing This Truth
1. Why might we fail to address situations that need addressing?

2. Have you failed to confront for any of these reasons? Which one? What was the result? What would you now hope to do differently?

3. Read 1 Peter 4:19 (NKJV). Sometimes silence is called for instead of confronting. What kinds of silences are there?

11

Be a People Helper

Getting to Know You
   What is one thing you appreciate about your mother and/or father?

Review Thoughts to Remember (Page 236)

Between Linx Practicing and Journaling (Page 236)
   Paul uses five principles in confronting: (1) affirm, (2) state what is wrong, (3) state how to correct the wrong, (4) explain the consequences if it is not corrected, and (5) expect accountability—a report. In more minor cases one may not use all five principles, but always affirm before addressing the situation. Write how you recently addressed an issue, big or small, and what the results were.

DAY 1 (PAGES 239-243 IN TEXTBOOK)

1. Read again the scriptures (page 239) that remind us we are all to encourage, love, care for, and strengthen one another. Which one is most meaningful to you?

2. What is a good description of a mentor?

The Ministry of Reconciliation
3. According to 2 Corinthians 5:19, what is God's plan for each of us? What are the three areas of reconciliation?

4. Our over-all goal in helping people is to communicate hope (Romans 15:13). How does God give hope to His children?

Day 2 (Pages 243-248)

Three Simple Ways to Be a People Helper
1. In what ways have you been a minister of encouragement, comfort, cheer, or love?

2. Think of people with whom you associate—work, family, friends. Whom will you plan to encourage as you are studying these principles of people-helping?

3. Read Proverbs 11:25. What happens to you when you reach out to refresh or encourage others?

4. People especially want to be affirmed in their work or ministry. Recall a time when someone affirmed you in this way and tell how it made you feel.

Day 3 (Pages 248-254)

Prerequisites for People-Helping
1. Read James 5:16; Psalm 139:23–24; and Proverbs 15:31–33. Why do you think that one of the prerequisites for people-helping is to be willing to see and admit your faults?

2. Recall the lady who prayed, "Lord, reveal to me my secret faults." What were the four relationship-damaging attitudes (blind spots) the Lord made her aware of? What happened when she began to change?

3. Review the other attitudes that can hinder good relationships. Which ones do you feel the Lord has helped you to overcome?

4. Do you feel it's possible that you might have some blind spots? Would you be willing to ask the Lord to show you any attitudes that might hinder relationships?

Day 4 (Pages 254-257)

1. Review the five suggested ways we can discover our offensive actions or attitudes. Which do you feel the Lord uses for you the most?

2. Would you share how you have used or experienced any of these?

3. Read Galatians 6:1 (AMP). What does it mean to be "Spirit controlled?"

4. On a scale of 1 to 10 (10 being the most) how do you rate the amount of talking you do in ordinary conversation?

   How do you rate the amount of listening you usually do?

Day 5 (Pages 258-261)

1. Read Galatians 6:1 (AMP). What is meant by being a humble learner?

2. What does it mean to "be nonpharisaical?"

3. Look over the entire list of "Prerequisites for People-Helping." In which areas do you do well?

   In which areas do you see a need for growth in your life? How can you incorporate these into your life?

12

Guides for People-Helping

Getting to Know You

What is one skill you possess that no one in your group may know about?

Review Thoughts to Remember (Page 261)

Between Linx Practicing and Journaling (Page 261)

As you review "Be Willing to See and Admit Your Faults" (pages ??), ask the Lord to reveal to you one of your blind spots. Is this blind spot giving an impression of a know-it-all attitude? Write an example of the way you displayed one of these negative attitudes this week. Tell how you became aware of it and what you did about it.

DAY 1 (PAGES 263-265 IN TEXTBOOK)

Job's Miserable Comforters

1. Read Job 2:11–13. What three things did Job's comforters do that were right?

2. Tell of an experience when someone comforted you in one of these ways.

3. What is a thought or two from the quote from Eugene Peterson that strikes you as especially noteworthy?

4. Note in Job 16:2 where Job calls these men "miserable comforters." What are some ways we are prone to become miserable comforters?

Day 2 (Pages 265-268)

1. Read Job 42:7–9. What did God say about the answers the "miserable comforters" gave?

2. How do we try to "fix" people and thus join the ranks of miserable comforters?

3. In essence the purpose of *Linx: Women Connecting with Women* is to help us avoid being miserable comforters. Instead, describe what we are to be like in our relationships with others.

4. God was a refuge for Job. In Job 16:7–11 notice how Job felt free to pour out all his angry thoughts and feelings to the Lord. How does his tone change in verses 19–21? What are several titles he calls God here?

Day 3 (Pages 268-270)

1. How does Oswald Chambers caution us about judging others?

2. In what ways did the three "friends" not understand Job?

3. Read Job 16:2–5. Job declared that if they were in his place he wouldn't speak as they spoke, but rather he would _____ and _____ them.

4. What else did they do wrong?

Day 4 (Pages 270-275)

Guides for People-Helping
1. What important principle of people-helping do James 1:19 and Proverbs 18:13 emphasize?

2. When we listen to someone, what are we communicating to him/her?

3. Read the *Joy and Strength* quote on page 271. How have some "listened" to you, but disappointed you or failed to communicate to you their interest in and concern for you?

4. How do Proverbs 18:13, 15, 17 help us "hear what they say."

Day 5 (Pages 275-279)

1. What are three basic things we should listen for when trying to help one who has come for our help?

2. What do we mean by "listen without condemnation?"

3. Which of the seven *Listen's* under "Guides for People-Helping" (pages 270-279) do you feel you need to give attention to?

4. Can you give an experience out of your life when someone really listened to you and comforted you by their careful listening more than by their words?

13

More Guides for People-Helping

Getting to Know You

If you had one week of vacation in which to recharge your physical and emotional batteries, where would you go to rest, relax, and get rejuvenated?

Review Thoughts to Remember (Page 279)

Between Linx Practicing and Journaling (Page 279)
1. Pray the suggested scripture prayer each day this week (textbook page 279).

2. Work at really listening to each of your family members or close friends this week. What were their responses? How did that make you feel?

Day 1 (Pages 281-284 in textbook)

Guides for People-Helping, Continued
1. Review the first seven "Guides for People-Helping" from chapter 12.

2. Why is it important to listen for the real problem?

3. Why is it important to listen for their own conclusions?

4. Why are periods of silence important?

5. Write a definition of "conscience."

DAY 2 (PAGES 284-288)

1. What is a weak conscience?

2. What is a legalistic conscience?

3. In helping people, how are we to be sensitive to their conscience in the issue?

Day 3 (Pages 288-291)

1. What instruction do you find in Proverbs 11:13 and 20:19?

2. What benefit is it to listen so you can ask careful questions at proper times?

3. What were the two brief questions Jesus asked the men on the road to Emmaus to get them to share their thoughts and feelings? (See Luke 24:17–24.)

4. Read through the list of possible questions you might ask at proper times to familiarize yourself with them. Have you had opportunity to use any of these?

Day 4 (Pages 291-296)

1. Why is it so helpful to give a person some projects?

2. What projects have you found helpful for yourself?

3. Is there one of the suggested projects that you feel you could profit from? Which one?

4. What are some ways you might drop a stone of encouragement in the water and see the ripples circling on and on? Or, how have you already started some ripples?

Day 5 (Pages 296-302)

Power for the People Helper
1. Read the promises of the Lord's help, page 297. Write out one that you especially want to remember and to claim.

2. What are five indicators of God's will?

3. What is the twofold purpose of *Linx, Women Connecting with Women?*

4. What is God calling you to do? Will you step out and trust Him?

14

Helping People in Crisis

Getting to Know You
   What was the nicest thing someone did for you when you had a need?

Review Thoughts to Remember (Page 301)

Between Linx Practicing and Journaling (Page 301)
1. Review the fourteen points under the importance of listening. Which ones do you feel you need to work on the most?

2. Speak some words of encouragement to each family member this week. Jot down what you said and their response.

3. Write a note or call a friend to encourage her. Ask her to go out for a cup of coffee or for a walk. Learn to take risks, initiate, and go beyond your comfort zone. Write what you did.

DAY 1 (PAGES 303-309 IN TEXTBOOK)

1. Write two things that made Mrs. Owl and Mrs. Pelican "miserable comforters."

2. Read 2 Corinthians 1:2–4. What are some things we might do to be the comfortable comforters that God wants us to be?

3. Share a time when someone was a "miserable comforter" to you. Describe the situation (trial, pain), their words, and how you felt toward them, toward yourself, toward God or all of these.

4. Share a time when you were anxious or in pain and a person was "God with skin on" (a comforting comforter) to you. Describe the situation (trial, pain), their words, and how you felt toward them, yourself, or God, or all of these.

Understanding and Applying the Crisis Cycle
1. Share a time in your life when you were in a time of crisis. How did you go through the negative phases? Did your thoughts eventually accept and seek God's wisdom in the hardship? Explain.

DAY 2 (PAGES 309-311)

General Guidelines for Helping People in Crisis
2. What are some things we can do to help people in a time of crisis?

3. What are some practical things others could have done to help you through a crisis?

Helping People in a Specific Crisis
4. What could help us as we seek to be God with skin on to someone who has just lost a dear one?

5. Why is it important to find a support person or group?

DAY 3 (PAGES 311-315)

Helping Children of Divorce
1. In helping a child of divorce, why is it important to emphasize that he is not to blame for the divorce?

2. What are some helpful things you could do for those suffering grief or loss?

3. What did the first visitor to Joseph Bayly do that made him wish that he'd go away?

4. What did Joseph Bayly's second visitor do that caused him to hate to see him go?

Day 4 (Pages 316-319)

The Painful Experience of a Wayward Adult Child
1. The wrong approach is to:

2. The right approach is to:

3. Though we can't expect immediate answers to prayer sometimes, what can we expect God to do? (Isaiah 61:3 and Ecclesiastes 3:11)

4. Why is it important to relinquish your hold on the adult child?

Day 5 (Pages 320-323)

Six Simple Suggestions for People-Helping
1. Think through a recent helping encounter with someone. Did you put any of these six suggestions into practice? Explain.

2. Share how someone comforted you in a time of crisis.

3. Choose a verse of hope and promise. Write it here and memorize it.

4. What is your commitment to reach out to others in the days ahead? Are you planning to join with one or more women for a ministry of encouragement, support, or mentoring? Write here what you plan to do.

Free Indeed

(Sung to the tune of "We Will Glorify")

Free to nourish others with God's love,
Helping them their load to bear;
With a listening ear show grace and truth,
Let them know you really care.

I must freely draw upon His love
So my needs are met in Him;
Then in glad obedience I will find
Joy and peace will come from Him.

Though we're scarred by sin and hurts of life,
We can choose to grow through pain;
Free to love, forgive, and hope again,
For with God it's not in vain.

Free to hear His voice of love and grace—
Calm and peace my fears erase;
Having thoughts full of His words of truth;
Help my heart-eyes see His face.

Understanding where my lines exist—
That which God has giv'n to me—
Frees me to extend a helping hand;
From oppression I'm set free.

Free to nourish others with God's love,
Helping them their load to bear;
With a listening ear show grace and truth,
Let them know you really care.

Leader's Notes

General Helps

Discussion groups offer opportunity for each woman to clarify the concepts in her own mind. By verbalizing and restating the principles in her own words, truths begin to become her own. The group members will be encouraging one another in the practical details of applying truth to specific, real-life situations, which is our over-all goal.

As leader, be enthusiastic about the biblical truths you are studying and about what the Lord can and will do in the life of each person. Do all you can to create a warm, friendly atmosphere where even strangers will feel at home and look forward to returning. Make it your goal to have a ready smile and a kind response in each contact.

With a spirit of humility expect the Lord to teach you along with the group. Don't expect to be "the expert" or the one who has all the answers. And remember, the more willing you are to open up and share from your own life, the more willing the group will be.

Plan ahead and keep within your advertised time limits. Provide a prepared place—calm, neat, well-lighted, and comfortably arranged. Above all, pray for each member—for open minds and hearts to receive God's truth; for clear, practical application to life; and for eager response to God in commitment and trust.

Suggestions for Weekly Meetings

Each participant will need both the textbook and the *Study Guide*. Since you may not be able to give the books out until your first meeting, we suggest studying chapter 1 together, answering the questions as you go through the book. More detailed helps are provided for the leader for chapter 1. But do encourage them to read chapter 1 on their own at home during the week before working on chapter 2.

To begin each meeting use the "Getting to Know You" question to give the women opportunity to tell a bit about themselves each week. As the weeks go by, this will be an important step in really getting to know more about each other and encouraging warm, helpful relationships.

In two or three sentences recall the content of the previous chapter and review the "Thoughts to Remember." Have several share from their "Between Linx Practicing and Journaling" project.

Introduce today's study with two or three sentences that give the main truth emphasized in the chapter. Spend 45 minutes to an hour in discussion of the chapter, using the *Study Guide* questions to guide you through it. Don't be afraid of periods of silence as the women are thinking. Draw answers from the group and try to avoid giving your own answers very often. Call attention to the succinct chapter summary as given in the "Thoughts to Remember," and urge the women to write these on a card and memorize both the verse and the statement. Conclude with prayer.

Assign the next chapter and remind them to work on the "Practicing and Journaling" during the week.

If you have a group larger than ten or twelve, it would be good to divide into smaller groups for the discussion time. Then, if you like, bring the groups together and give a short wrap-up. "Suggestions for Wrap-Up" are given for each week.

Practical Helps for the Leader

Unless you are all well known to each other, use name tags every week and work at using and remembering names. Speak loudly enough so everyone can hear.

Be gentle but firm in dealing with any disagreements. If someone seems to be upset, graciously move on to another question. Try not to let one person dominate the time. Do not embarrass a shy person by calling on her, but do your best to include her in the group. Try to encourage everyone who shares. Each needs the assurance they are "okay," or some will hesitate to share more.

Remember, some may be going through a rough time as they face lifetime failures and as they see more and more of God's way. They need your support and love. Yours may be the purest human love they have ever known. Do everything you can to make them feel special.

Week by Week
Page numbers refer to textbook unless otherwise noted.

CHAPTER 1

If you are distributing the books at this first meeting, you will want to give some specific guidance through the questions as you answer them together from the textbook. Suggestions are given here:

Needed: Safe People, Safe Places
1. Read aloud the story of Verna's dad who yearned for safe people and safe places. The uncle gave no pay and no praise, was critical and harsh.

    A. Verna's dad's dad let the uncle take advantage of him.
    B. Our soul's hunger for justice, respect, affirmation, understanding, and connection. How were these not met in this situation?
    C. See "Our Deep Soul Hunger for Connection."
    D. Our two key words are *equipping* and *connecting.*

Key Word: Connecting
1. Let the women share their thoughts. Also see "Our General Need for Affirmation."
2. List together the directives Paul gives in these verses. Also have someone look up and read Hebrews 10:24–25.
3. Read aloud Hannah's story on page 16. What was it that helped Hannah? Verna gave grace by listening, giving very little advice, giving her time and acceptance, loving, and not judging.
4. See "Our Confused and Twisted Thinking." Release from the results of legalism, from false guilt and shame. Release to understand her boundaries, rights, and responsibilities.

Key Word: Equipping
1. Connections will be much deeper and more effective. Preparing women is vital. Preparation must come before vital connections can take place. Call attention to "Why Do Christians Shoot Their Wounded" and Verna's visit with "Mrs. Mentor" (page 21). Some would-be mentors are well meaning but too confident. Some are too reluctant—feeling too inadequate to become involved on any level.

2. Read together Titus 2:3–4. Titus was to teach the older women how to live. Then they could teach the younger women how to live.
4. Leader, you might share first in order to give the others time to think.
5. Let the women think about this and mark the line. Some may be willing to share their answer and why they rated themselves as they did.

The Work of Encouragement
1. Leader, you might use the story of Janelle to introduce this. (Page 20)
2. Some of the women may be able to answer this. Do not pressure for answers. This may be a new thought to many.

A Challenge to Get Involved
1. Draw attention to Isaiah 61:1–4, mentioning the various ways we can be involved in what God is doing.
2. It requires *faith* and *action* and major *adjustments* in our *thinking*.
3. Moses needed to change his thinking about himself and God. Take note of how God led Him in this process. Verna had to realize God could make her adequate, and she rested in His promise in John 15:16.
4. Leader, perhaps you could share your own experience.

Thoughts to Remember
Read together the "Thoughts to Remember" at the end of chapter 1. Doing this each week will solidify the main thrust of the study for that week.

For Next Week
Assign chapter 2 in the *Linx: Women Connecting with Women* textbook and the questions in the *Study Guide*.

CHAPTER 2

You might bring some samples of humorous cards and supportive comments. What encouragement even a humorous card or one with a simple message can be!

Day 1
Not all of the nourishment Jesus and Paul dispensed tasted good, but it was necessary for the growth of those involved.

Day 2

Draw attention to "Nourishment Direct from God," page 36. Read Psalm 142:1–5. How can we apply this to our own lives?

Day 3

Additional question: What do women need from other women more than "being fixed"? (Someone to listen to, believe in, accept, and seek to understand them.) Why and in what ways is this more helpful?

Day 4

2. Additional question: In what four areas might someone need an advocate to defend them?

Day 5

Complete this section by discussing "Balancing This Truth." (page 50)

Suggestions for Wrap-Up for Chapter 2

Review what it means to be "God with skin on"—Advocate, Paraclete, Refuge, again explaining each. Read 1 Peter 5:1–5 (Phillips is good). Note the warning not to lord it over the flock, but to be examples of true Christian living. From Ezekiel 34:1–16, note the characteristics of the faithless and the faithful shepherds of the flock. End with an illustration as to how you have been "God with skin on" to someone or someone to you. Give some suggestions as to how they can be such to others.

Read together "Thoughts to Remember" and challenge them to do the "Practicing and Journaling" for this week. Assign chapter 3 for next week.

Sing: "We Will Glorify," verses 1 and 2.

Chapter 3

Take a few minutes to review last week's "Thoughts to Remember," page 52, and have several report on the "Practicing and Journaling" project they did this past week.

Day 1

3. Our empty spots are to be filled with God's love and the love of people. Affirmation, encouragement, recognition, unconditional acceptance, and continual approval are all part of that love we are to share with

one another. These help, on the human side, to fill our emotional love tank.

Day 2

1. God's original plan was for the family to meet our nourishment needs on the human level. The family is the first and most important "filling station." Sin marred the plan and that sin principle within still plagues us. We tend toward being selfish, independent people with an "I-want-my-way" attitude. This causes struggles and unhappiness when we let it have its way in our lives.

4. Jesus ate and slept, walked and worked. He did not neglect Himself even while giving of Himself sacrificially to others in His travels.

Day 3

2. Jesus spent time in prayer, and He was also nourished by doing the will of God.

3. Leader, make sure the women in your group understand what it means to become a child of God. Study together the scriptures given.

4. Discuss some specific helps for getting nourishment from God. Talk about a plan—time, place, methods, etc.

Day 4

2. God lavished Adam and Eve with an environment that provided soul nourishment. A garden—pleasant and good for food, a river to water it, even gold and precious stones. He gave them work to do, limits for security, opportunity for creative thinking, and to cap it all off, companionship.

Day 5

2. The Bible says that selfishness and self-centeredness are to be denied, but we do need relationship with others. My motive lets me know if I'm being selfish or wise.

Suggestions for Leader's Wrap-Up for Chapter 3

Give some personal illustrations from your life or the lives of others who felt it was selfish to meet their own needs. Or, of someone who tried to substitute other things in the place of God as their primary source of nourishment. Expand on how Jesus, the disciples, and/or apostles nourished themselves and/or reached out for nourishment from others.

Sing: "We Will Glorify," and "Free Indeed," verses 1 and 2 (see *Study Guide* page 75).

CHAPTER 4

Day 1

At the end of this section call attention to sources other than the family that cause malnourishment in the child (page 86).

Day 2

3. Follow-up question: What can we learn from the model of Joseph's life?

Day 3

1. Luke 17:3 and 1 Peter 4:8 give both sides of the truth or the balance of truth. Sometimes it is right to confront; other times we should simply let love cover that sin.

Day 4

4. As you walk more and more according to the Spirit, you will experience wonderful freedom, and the process of healing can begin to take place. Read Jeremiah 29:11 for the group.

Day 5

1. We don't need to go back into our past and try to dig up everything, but we do need to be open and ready to learn from the Lord through whatever "teacher" He has for us—a person, a circumstance, His Word, or the "still, small voice" of the Holy Spirit in our hearts.
5. Who is the one who opposes renewing our minds according to God's truth? What are we to do? (1 Peter 5:6-9; James 4:7)

Suggestions for Leader's Wrap-Up

Highlight the thoughts about Joseph and his forgiveness of his brothers. Pray during the week before that the women will honestly let the Holy Spirit examine their hearts to see if there is someone they need to forgive. Encourage them to purpose to do so now. Let them know you are available to help them follow through if they would like your support.

You might recap the thoughts under "The Need to Change Our Twisted Thinking" (page 98). Use the suggested Scriptures and emphasize the importance of taking wrong thoughts captive and renewing the mind. Be aware that this is a process and that the enemy will oppose. Share what 1 Peter 5:6–9 and James 4:7–8 say about that.

Sing: "Free Indeed," verses 1–3.

CHAPTER 5

Day 1
1. Emphasize that my problem comes not from what has happened to me but from my beliefs or self-talk about the event. Therefore, to change my feelings I don't have to change the event or the person, but I must change my self-talk about the event or person.

Day 2
1. Leader, can you give an illustration out of your life when you were saying negative things to yourself about yourself or about others and how you felt as a result?

Day 3
2. An additional question: What are some of the thoughts of the one who is perfectionistic in tasks? How might these be changed?

Day 5
3. Emphasize the importance of committing ourselves to discover and correct our wrong conclusions and distorted views, replacing them with truth, because the "truth will set you free." (John 8:32)

Suggestions for Wrap-Up:
1. Other Biblical references relating to self-talk are: Psalm 73 and Jeremiah the prophet in Lamentations 3. You could share from one or both of these.
2. Discuss the section on reconciling good and bad in the world, in others, and in ourselves. Refer to John 8:3–11 for an example from Scripture. Bring out the benefits of journaling one's feelings and re-emphasize the summary of reconciling good and bad.

Sing: "Free Indeed," verses 1–4.

CHAPTER 6

Day 3
4. At the end of this section read the story of the woman expecting her fourth child and discuss the questions on page 132.

Suggestions for Wrap-Up:
1. Read the three paragraphs from, *If God Is in Control, Why Is My World Falling Apart* on page 126. What does the typical western Christian do to try to find a "quick fix" that might solve the problem? Why do we have so much soul anguish and struggle in this world?
2. Take another look at Job and repeat and expand on some thoughts about him.
3. Expand on some of the scripture references to people "talking to themselves" given at the end of "Practicing and Journaling."

Sing: "Free Indeed," verses 1–4.

CHAPTER 7

Day 2
1. Follow-up question: What gives evidence that Jesus respected and protected Mary's boundaries?
3. Additional questions: What are some illustrations of violated boundaries that you have observed? Or, what is some common twisted thinking of some whose boundaries have been violated?

Day 5
1. Make sure the group understands that setting limits does not mean that you are not showing love to the other person. There is a place for tough love in Christian relationships.
2. Graciously drawing proper boundaries results in great freedom and an increase of love and respect for one another.

Suggestions for Wrap-Up:
1. Expand on the statement, "One significant way of nourishing others with bold love is to help them draw boundaries." This could be illustrated with Glenna and her parents, page 152.

2. You might want to give more teaching about rights—the freedom to exercise or to waive our rights—from 1 Corinthians 9.

Sing: "Free Indeed," verses 1, 2, 5.

CHAPTER 8

Day 1
4. You might also look together at the "Do's" in "Guidelines for Drawing Boundaries." Think about which one you need to give most attention to.

Day 4
1. Have three people summarize these three reasons.

Day 5
4. Additional question: Can you think of a time when you *didn't* draw a boundary and you should have? Describe the situation and what you could have done differently.

Suggestions for Wrap-Up
1. Share times when Jesus drew boundaries, John 12:1–8; Luke 4:1–13, 42–43; John 21:19–22.
2. Read through and discuss Candace's experience using some of these questions:
   1) What were some of Candace's wrong assumptions?
   2) Where did she fail to draw boundaries?
   3) Where were her boundaries violated by others?
   4) Why did she let this happen?
   5) What factors gave her the "serve, serve, do, do" way of life?
   6) What was some of her self-talk and how did it affect her feelings?
   7) How did she come to realize that it isn't wrong to say no?
   8) What difference did it make in her life after she learned to say no?

Sing: "Free Indeed," verses 1, 2, 5.

CHAPTER 9

Day 5

Call attention to Romans 12:18. If the other person won't hear or admit his wrong and harmony cannot be restored, you are free if you have taken care of what is your responsibility

Suggestions for Wrap-Up

1. Talk more about the "Jesus Way," using scripture to illustrate each of the three ways.
2. Review the dialogues of mother and Julie. Compare mother's first method of responding with her "Jesus way" responses.
3. Read and evaluate Rae Ann's story of her Prince Charming by using these questions:
   1) What was her husband's response when she confronted him with these "hidden things"?
   2) What was her response to Sam's confession and repentance?
   3) Several times she became suicidal. What factors encouraged this desire?
   4) What was Sam's response when any discussion or heated arguments came up?
   5) Why didn't she want to let any one know what was going on in their marriage?
   6) How did she come to the point of being willing to release the secret, face the issue, and determine to get professional help?
   7) How did time away help her? What did she learn from it?
   8) In considering moving back, she needed some evidence that this time his change was real. What did she do to help determine this?

Sing: "Free Indeed," verses 1, 3, 5.

CHAPTER 10

Day 5

3. Emphasize that we need the Holy Spirit's discernment and often the wise counsel of godly people to know when to lovingly confront or when to respond in silence.

Suggestions for Wrap-Up
1. Further analyze the dialogue between Jana and Rita. Some ideas: 1) Notice how Jana responded in the "Jesus way." 2) Jana took the initiative to try to heal the breach in fellowship. 3) What was Rita's response to Jana's attempt to be kind and understanding? 4) Was the situation resolved and the friendship restored? (No. That is sometimes reality. "If it is possible, as far as it depends on you, live at peace with everyone." Romans 12:18)
2. Review the "Guidelines for Confronting": 1) Decide why you need to confront. 2) Choose the place and time. 3) Study how to confront Paul's way. End with some thoughts from the closing paragraphs and the suggested scriptures under "Balancing This Truth," page 233.

Introduce Linx Friendships Idea

Encourage the women to think about developing a *Linx* Friendship when this study ends—a Friendship Linx Duo, Friendship Linx Triad, or Friendship Linx Quad. They could meet together as twos, threes, or fours for a five- or six-week review of the material covered. Or, they could do another brief study. Or, just get together for a chat and prayer. This is a good way to go deeper in connecting with one other person or a few others. Encourage them to pray about this and take some risks in connecting with some other ladies for support and mentoring.

Sing: "Free Indeed," verses 1–3.

CHAPTER 11

Day 1
4. Have several look up and read: Romans 15:13; Exodus 33:14; 1 Corinthians 10:13; Philippians 4:19

Day 2
3. You might have some share how they have been refreshed by refreshing others.

Day 3

Ask, Have you ever felt wounded and shot down because of someone's relationship-damaging attitude? Explain.

Suggestions for Wrap-Up

Emphasize that a prerequisite for people-helping is a willingness to see and admit faults. Review the ways we might become aware of faults. Read and give some comments on the story of Nathan and David (2 Samuel 12). How was his sin revealed? What difference did it make in him when he faced and confessed it? (See Psalms 32 and 51.) What happened to the rich young ruler who refused to face his faults (Luke 18:18–24). Think what benefit it was to Joseph, his brothers, and his father when they were finally ready to see their faults, their sin, Genesis 44–45.

Sing: "Free Indeed."

CHAPTER 12

Day 4

4. Read Proverbs 17:27–28 and call attention to the importance of listening to build confidence by being quiet.

Day 5

1. In addition to these three basic things, what are some other things we can listen for?

Suggestions for Wrap-Up

More lessons from Job: What kind of man was he actually? What did God say about him? What did he prove himself to be after the tragedies? What kinds of answers and accusations did his miserable comforters make? What wrong assumptions were they building their case on? How did they violate some principles of good listening? Where did they err? What did God have to say to and about them in the end? What lessons can we learn from them?

Sing: "Free Indeed," verses 1–3.

CHAPTER 13

Day 1

1. Were you reminded this week of one of the seven "Listens"? How did you apply it?

Day 2

2. How does 1 Corinthians 8:9–12 help us with the gray areas of right and wrong?

Suggestions for Wrap-Up

1. You might review all the "Listens" and "Speaks" with some comments.
2. Focus on the power of the Holy Spirit to do the work in us. Review the promises given on page 297. Also: Philippians 4:13 (AMP); 2 Corinthians 9:8; Isaiah 41:10; Jeremiah 1:4–9. Tell how the Lord has empowered you.

Sing: "Free Indeed," verses 4–6.

CHAPTER 14

Day 3

Additional questions: What is Dr. Jeremiah's warning? (Page 315) What is meant by "Be Biblical in Your Response"?

Suggestions for Wrap-Up

1. Re-emphasize and summarize the points under "The Painful Experience of a Wayward Adult Child."
2. Remember God's plan is to transform, restore, rebuild, and renew (Isaiah 61:3–4), but He wants us to be His instruments through whom He can work. Keep in mind His words in Jeremiah 29:11, "'For I know the plans I have for you,' declares the Lord, 'plans to prosper you and not to harm you, plans to give you hope and a future.'" Call attention to how God wants us to be comforted (Isaiah 51:12) and to comfort (Isaiah 40:1; 2 Corinthians 1:3–4).
3. Perhaps read together Karen's experience, page 322.
4. Turn again to Isaiah 61:1–4, which gives God's plan: Jesus' mission and our mission in this world. "As you (Father) sent me into the world, I have sent them into the world" (John 17:18).

Sing: "Free Indeed."

Materials for Christian Growth Available from Enriched Living

Linx: Women Connecting with Women, $14.99—Equipping women for a life-changing ministry of friend-to-friend mentoring and people-helping. For personal or group study.

Study Guide for Linx: Women Connecting with Women, $5.99—A companion to the textbook for personal or group study. Includes Leader's Notes.

If God Is in Control, Why Is My World Falling Apart? $8.95—How is it possible to say that God is both sovereign and good? With gentle wisdom, Verna leads us to a place of unshakable trust that can joyfully assert, "God loves me and I can rest in His tender control."

You Are Very Special, $7.95—Practical, biblical helps to let God communicate to your heart that you are someone very special! "As my friends and I have been studying *You Are Very Special* together, I have finally come to know who I am in Christ and to believe that God really does love me! What freedom!"

Growth Guide, You Are Very Special, $2.25—Study guide for individual and group study.

Less Stress, More Peace, $9.00—Even though we are part of a stress-filled world, we have available to us a God-given handle for relieving, managing, and rising above daily stresses, and experiencing God's peace. Includes projects for personal or group study.

God's Promises of Peace, $1.95—A compilation of Scripture to help us rest in our loving Lord in every circumstance of life. Each of the 52 meditations emphasizes a different phase of peace. Excellent for memorizing Scripture.

Great gift for someone facing change, suffering, loneliness, rejection, sorrow, and need for guidance.

God's Pattern for Enriched Living, Workshop One, Textbook, $10.00—Making home a place of refuge, building a sense of worth, promoting open communication, learning to trust God when you cannot understand.

God's Pattern for Enriched Living, Workshop Two, Textbook, $10.00—Learning the fine art of Godly parenting—discipline, training, acceptance, respect, love, security.

Audio and video teaching programs are also available. Write for details.

To order

Linx:
Women Connecting with Women

textbooks and additional *Study Guides*
or any of the books listed on pages 91-92, call

1-800-917-BOOK

or write to:

Enriched Living
P. O. Box 3039
Kent, WA 98032-0221